Regulation

Regulation

Lord Loveday Ememe

Regulation

Lord Loveday Ememe 2

By Lord Loveday Ememe and available from Lulu and Amazon

The constitution and policing

Heresy

Starfleet

The Supernatural

Creation

Deterrence

Stalking

The media

Adam

Criminal Responsibility

The Wicked

Common Law

Racism

Regulation

www.lulu.com

Copyright© Lord Loveday Ememe 2015

The author asserts the moral right to be recognized as the author of this work.
ISBN: 978-1-326-53458-5

Regulation

Table of Contents

1. Uncivilized supernatural regulation

2. Civilized legal regulation

3. The State

4. Author's notes

5. Author's biography

6. Bibliography

Regulation

1. Uncivilized supernatural regulation

Regulation

The uncivilized supernatural regulation is a type of regulation with no clearly defined rules subject to the changing moods of supernatural beings, with the monitoring stalking effect. Only supernatural beings are privy to the new changes to the rules linked to this type of regulation or understand them even when these affect other species or races. Only supernatural beings are naturally equipped to handle the supernatural intrusion associated with this type of regulation and the punishments linked to this type of regulation only deter other species or races and not supernatural beings. The nature of the differences between the civil and supernatural constitutions confirms that the civil constitution is the subject or focus of this method of regulation.
There are two types of supernatural regulations, the direct political red regulation and the indirect political blue regulation. These regulations have been identified and categorized in the bible as angels and demons.
These regulations require the manipulation of supernatural powers and senses to create the need for them in the lives of the vulnerable including the civil noble constitution.
I am experiencing some health problems which would suggest that I am not allowed to write about my experiences, this will suggest that a supernatural being or supernatural beings believe that the tortured existence that has been forced on me unlawfully abominably is a joke or game to them, it is not a joke or game to me.
These supernatural political red and blue interferences referred to as regulations cumulate to make the lives of the

vulnerable including the civil noble constitution torturous, hell, unlawfully, this will inevitably trigger the civil noble constitution's sacred legal right of vengeance the condemnation to hell of the wicked, as described in the bible. They use these supernatural regulations to interfere with the vulnerable as if using a remote control to operate machinery, similar to using a gun to shoot at someone to make them move to the right or to move to the left. It is abominable that you can be on your own and attract these supernatural regulations if you sit or stand in a way that is not politically correct, it makes no difference if you are legally correct, if your behaviour is offensive to one or more of the political colours. This makes the civil noble constitution a mouse in a game for cats.

These political supernatural regulations operate under limited resources, racist conditions, in what are already hostile conditions each supernatural political group try to sabotage the efforts of the other in the life of the subject, the civil noble constitution.

These supernatural political regulations operate under a false reality, lies, limited resources, and the deliberate compromise of the sacred civil rights of the civil noble constitution to make the civil noble constitution directly or indirectly vulnerable or susceptible to the control of these supernatural political regulations.

These supernatural political lawless regulations require the undermining of the law, the civil noble constitution, which facilitates the fraud of misrepresenting the civil noble

constitution as either a ghost or medically disabled or an inanimate object or establishing political manipulative phantom relationships with the civil noble constitution.
These are categorized by common law as supernatural beings unlawfully casting spells on the civil noble constitution.
These political systems require claiming moral superiority over every other political group, any other system of government, any other race, this will also require the misuse of supernatural powers and senses to try to establish and maintain moral superiority.
Unfortunately these supernatural lawless regulations do not allow for any type of relationship between the civil and supernatural constitutions. They do not permit any type of social life for the civil noble constitution; the civil noble constitution is restricted to the life of a prisoner, a prisoner of these supernatural lawless regulations.
The supernatural methods of regulation undermine state services, they rather things are done or obtained supernaturally rather than done or obtained freely safely through the state.
These supernatural regulatory systems operate by undermining the confidence of the vulnerable; they thrive on the creation or manufacture of problems. The victims are manipulated with the misuse of supernatural powers and senses to always seek the approval of their supernatural oppressors. A type of psychological oppression or domination. These atrocities are going on while the supernatural oppressors are pretending officially to be legal

persons without supernatural powers and senses claiming superior mental and physical abilities over the civil noble constitution in a hostile lawless political system.

These supernatural regulations restrict the monarch, the civil noble constitution, to a constant state of arrest, a puppet, susceptible to supernatural political manipulations.

These supernatural political regulations leave the wellbeing, mental and physical, of the civil noble constitution, to the mercy of supernatural beings and not the predetermined sacred civil rights of the civil noble constitution, given the hostile unnatural or uncivilized sensitivity of the supernatural constitution this means unlawfully making the life of the civil noble constitution torturous.

These supernatural political regulations treat the civil noble constitution as a being not born of God, as criminally responsible, with no civil rights.

These supernatural political regulations create conditions unlawfully to treat the civil noble constitution as a childlike being, a juvenile delinquent, an object of ridicule.

The supernatural constitution is naturally hostile uncivilized and create hostile conditions to suit the supernatural constitution at the expense of law and order and at the expense of the mental and physical wellbeing of those different from them. These supernatural regulations have been specifically designed to accommodate the hostile nature of the supernatural constitution. Contacts, communications, plans, methods, goals or objectives etcetera have been designed by these supernatural regulations to be hostile to vulnerable beings that are not supernatural beings, to accommodate the hostile sadistic nature of the supernatural constitution.

Supernatural beings under these supernatural regulations delude the vulnerable, cast spells, into believing that processes or procedures or methods hide their unlawful supernatural constitutions and release them from the responsibilities or obligations associated with the supernatural constitution.

The supernatural lawless regulatory system encourages supernatural beings to take advantage of the limitations of the vulnerable by using confusion, the lack of clarity, insufficient facts, to invite danger into the lives of the vulnerable, including the life of the civil noble constitution. These supernatural lawless political regulations given the nature of the supernatural constitution can only operate on role play, role plays for reasons already stated in my previous books are beyond the capabilities of the civil noble constitution, the legally recognized person, and this suggests that role play as a method of regulation is wrong, unlawful. This also confirms that all deaths of supernatural beings are either fake or suicides or in the case of supernatural babies, murder. Although the pattern remains constant that supernatural babies will grow up to exhibit the same behavioural traits as the adults in this lawless culture, it is a possibility that with proper education in a lawful environment or system, will reverse the current trend of supernatural babies growing up to be barbaric, to misuse supernatural powers and senses in a civilized society and to undermine the role of the civil noble constitution as ruler. The key component of these supernatural political regulations is separation from the state, privatization, the undermining of the state or law and order. It is important to note that privatization or capitalism has a proper regulatory application, the protection of the civil nature of the civil noble constitution from supernatural alterations in order not to undermine the regulatory sensibility or judgment of the civil noble constitution, to protect and to maintain the legal status of the civil noble constitution. Lawful regulatory instructions are private to the civil noble constitution because of how the civil noble constitution has been constituted which has universal application. Privatization is being used by these supernatural political regulations as a revolutionary mechanism to undermine the regulatory functions of the state.

These supernatural political regulations use privatization to create inequality or unfairness, oppression or domination, poverty and lawlessness or racism.

Under these supernatural regulations privatization requires substandard products that are in regular need of repair and replacement to make privatization or capitalism viable.

These supernatural political regulations create conditions to allow supernatural beings to interfere with anybody supernaturally against their will, supernatural or civil beings. An example is eating, rather than eat when you are hungry, they create conditions to make sure you eat three times a day at specific times in a day or else you start experiencing some health problems. This takes away the pleasures or joys of eating.

The supernatural indirect political regulation, political blue, uses method, being methodical in an abusive way, for instance, illnesses that are supernatural phenomena, have to have lifespans and a method of treatment which are categorized by international legislations as torture. Illnesses or diseases are supernatural unnatural phenomena created by supernatural beings, referred to by these regulations as naturally occurring phenomena. All international and domestic legislations refer to illnesses or diseases and old age or ageing as natural, this is untrue; they are supernatural unnatural phenomena and violations of article 3 of the universal declaration of human rights and article 6 of the international convention on civil and political rights, the right to life.

These supernatural political regulations create problems to solve for each other, a type of job creation. Supernatural solutions are in most cases more traumatic than the problem. The political blues create a false moral standard which the political reds are happy to rebel against without appropriate solutions. The reds wreck the efforts of the blues, creating things for the blues to do, all these dramatics at the expense of real law and order.

These supernatural regulations' primary objective is the supremacy of the supernatural political constitution at the expense of law and order, they create conditions to feed the

Regulation

wicked sadistic nature of the supernatural constitution, this involves the regular torture of the vulnerable including the civil noble constitution. These torturous experiences are similar but worse than, in principle to, the story in a film, speed, fiction, with actor Keanu Reeves and actress Sandra Bullock, it was about an insane person played by Dennis Hopper who put a bomb on a bus, it was rigged to make sure that the bus cannot go below fifty five miles per hour, once it goes below fifty five miles per hour it will explode. This is how supernatural beings want the civil noble constitution to live, with supernatural phenomena like illnesses, ageing and death hanging over you, like being on death row. The civil noble constitution, given the differences between the civil and supernatural constitutions, is not criminally responsible yet under these supernatural regulations has been sentenced to death.

It has been established in the bible that the civil noble constitution has been constituted to be naturally allergic to supernaturalism or supernatural methods or supernatural manifestations, when Lady Eve was created for Lord Adam; Lord Adam was shielded from witnessing the supernatural creation of Lady Eve. Yet these supernatural regulations are based on supernatural methods or manifestations, angels and demons. Supernatural beings under these regulations try to fend off some supernatural attacks on the civil noble constitution by supernatural methods on the one hand and on the other support these lawless supernatural regulations, it is like building a house on quicksand.

These supernatural regulations offer supernatural beings the opportunity to cater to the sadistic need to power trip to have the power of life and death over other life forms that are regarded as lower life forms by these racist regulations. They want you to feel the effect of having the power of life and death by toying with your heath taking you to the brink of death and back again, this is the natural trait of the supernatural constitution. After the conspiracy to create the effect they feel the need to establish a relationship with the victim and pretend that nothing happened at the same time revelling in the effect they had created.

No amount of money or glitter can mask the identities of real demons; all that glitters is not gold. These regulations try to create false impressions that angels are really demons and demons are really angels, this is nonsense or bullshit. It is correct to refer to a supernatural criminal as a demon because demon is another word for criminal, only supernatural beings are capable of criminal behaviour if they misuse their supernatural powers and senses. Both the biblical angels and demons fall short of the law abiding behaviour expected from supernatural beings.

The timing of the creation of Lady Eve as an afterthought for the pleasure of Lord Adam after the confirmation of Lord Adam as ruler serves an important regulatory purpose, the subsequent events leading to the undermining of the authority of Lord Adam and the subsequent creation of lawlessness confirm the failures of supernatural regulations. Supernatural political regulations are based on lies, the deception of the vulnerable; they can only operate in a false reality on deception or lies. The determination has been made that supernatural beings cannot disassociate their supernatural powers and senses from their supernatural constitutions, this means that to lie to or to deceive the civil noble constitution is categorized by common law as unlawfully casting a spell or casting spells on the civil noble constitution with severe punishments for the offenders. These supernatural political regulations enforce the unlawful separation from the state by deliberately misapplying the law, the Christian teachings, by the persecution of the civil noble constitution by creating systems and laws that establish lawlessness.

These supernatural political regulations, lawlessness, operate in the same way as the gang culture; you have to be compromised in order not to be a threat to other gang members. The civil noble constitution is obviously a threat to these lawless regulations so has to be compromised. The dumb criminal syndrome associated with supernatural criminal behaviour is revealed when supernatural beings believe the civil noble constitution can be compromised, set up while under their spell. The existence of the differences between the civil and supernatural constitutions means that the possibility of criminal behaviour from the civil noble constitution does not exist. Supernatural beings' manipulations of supernatural powers and senses can create the illusion of criminal behaviour which will not hold up to proper legal scrutiny. The comedy is the revealing attempts by supernatural beings to dominate the civil noble constitution by using or making references to supernatural set ups of the civil noble constitution.

Unfortunately under these supernatural political regulations what are natural interests for the civil noble constitution are used as weapons to harm the civil noble constitution. A natural interest, companionship, which is a civil right, is denied the civil noble constitution in direct and indirect ways, treating the natural interest as if an interest from a slave or a second class citizen. This natural interest is obstructed by compromising the civil noble constitution physically to make the experience unpleasant; it is also obstructed with threats of supernatural phenomena referred to as diseases or illnesses. Food, drinks etcetera are made unpleasant for the civil noble constitution.

Under these supernatural political regulations it is the practice to regulate the legal rather than the illegal; it maintains the godlike effect of the supernatural constitution. An example are the alterations to films and music, legally recognized and described products and services, rather than correct the alterations to make the products and services legal again for the legal consumer, the civil noble constitution, they choose to stop the legal consumer exercising the legal right to use these products and services by supernaturally interfering with the health of the legal consumer as if the legal consumer is doing something wrong or about to do something wrong.

If one person of a civil noble constitution and a million

supernatural beings are on an island, with a lot of lawless activities, breaches of the peace, by supernatural beings, they, one million supernatural beings, will only regulate the lawful activities of the one civil noble person as if criminally responsible, in order to maintain the godlike effect at the expense of peace and security.

These supernatural political regulations create problems in the lives of the vulnerable, damage to property supernaturally, health problems, financial insecurity, to gain access to the vulnerable, especially in circumstances where the vulnerable avoids contact with supernatural beings. If you are of a civil noble constitution, righteous, you are constantly plagued with these political problems by demons. They want to blackmail you directly or indirectly with these political problems. They have different political uses for these political problems in the lives of the righteous, the cumulative effect is to make the lives of the righteous hell or torturous unlawfully.

These supernatural political regulations operate under inhumane living conditions because supernatural beings take for granted the needs of those that are different from them because of their supernatural powers and senses.

Under these political regulations, criminal investigations only rely on evidence of the act, actus reus, and not the intent, mens rea. This allows the majority of supernatural crimes to be committed and the vulnerable including the civil noble constitution to be at the mercy of supernatural beings and not the law. These regulations allow crimes committed under the influence of spells and hypnosis, where the vulnerable are used as mediums by supernatural beings, to go undetected or not investigated, the mediums are blamed and punished for supernatural crimes.

This crucial component to the establishment of a crime, mens rea, malice aforethought, supernatural powers and senses, is ignored, treated as irrelevant under these regulations to maintain unlawful supernatural supremacy over the civil noble constitution.

Inhumane contacts or communications or living conditions or eating habits or foods etcetera are caused by the nature of the supernatural constitution which has been the indirect standard used by supernatural beings pretending to be of civil constitutions. The natural perception or assessment of supernatural beings, the unlawful standard, is the reason organized barbarisms are presented as civilizations. This mentality accounts for barbarisms referred to as political systems of government. It is important to note that another word for regulation is protection, a contradiction under these supernatural political regulations.

When somebody says that they are going to teach you a lesson, attack you, it is derived from the wicked practices of supernatural beings; they create problems or confusion and traumatize you with their chosen method or methods to correct the problems they had created. This caters to the nature of the sadistic, inhuman. Associations with supernatural beings by other life forms are not sort or offered, their trait is to harm, to create reasons they can pass

Regulation

off as legitimate to toy with other life forms unlawfully, supernaturally.

What will barbarians do with the arrival of a baby or the conquering of a village or country or come into contact with someone who is not a barbarian? It is to convert them to their way of life, barbarism. The nature of the barbarian is reflected in the system or systems of government or regulation they choose. The afterlife they advocate will reflect the nature of the barbarian. Death, illnesses and ageing will be incorporated into the culture of the barbarian. These forms of torture are suited to the hostile living conditions preferred by barbarians. They fit into the violent lifestyles preferred by barbarians.

To be violent is to be better in order to socialize, to toughen up to be a suitable companion for the barbarian. This is the function of the uncivilized supernatural political regulation.

Regulation

2. Civilized legal regulation

Regulation

What is civilized legal regulation? It is simply the standard. It is another way to refer to a king or ruler or law lord. The civilized legal regulation is the civil noble constitution. The delicate nature of the civil noble constitution regulates the behaviour of the supernatural constitution. The simplicity of the purpose or function of a real ruler makes a mockery of the redefinition of this sacred office by supernatural beings to suit their wicked constitutions at the expense of peace and security.

The requirement of supernatural beings under the civil legal regulation is to uphold the law, to uphold the rule of law; this means the supremacy of the civil noble constitution.

The civil noble constitution as the standard determines how information is provided, it should not be confusing, misleading, given for the purpose of causing harm to the recipient. To misinform or to mislead the civil noble constitution has been categorized by common law as casting a spell or casting spells on the civil noble constitution, this is considered a serious criminal offence with severe consequences for the offenders.

Information or education cannot be provided as if the recipient is a supernatural being who is expected to be aware already of the information being provided. In some cases or some issues, things have to be explained to supernatural beings properly because there are some civil issues that are beyond the scope of understanding of the supernatural constitution.

The civilized legal regulation requires that all supernatural

Regulation

beings must be regulated; this means that they are required to behave appropriately, responsible use of their supernatural powers and senses. This requires an international police service, the reconstitution of the United Nations, all countries must harmonize their laws to comply with the prime directive, the civil noble constitution is the law, standard and ruler. This international police service must not be obstructed, has to operate with the understanding that the supernatural constitution extends beyond national and planetary boundaries and the police service must respond to this reality for regulatory purposes.

This is consistent with the sacred determination made that the meek shall inherit the planet, the meek, the civil noble constitution, has dominion over this planet.

The harmonization of national and planetary laws to comply with the prime directive, the civil noble constitution is ruler or the standard, is as a consequence of the nature of the supernatural constitution, the supernatural powers and senses, the threat to the security of the civil noble constitution.

The civilized legal regulation regulates supernatural beings, to ensure that they do not force themselves indirectly or directly on anyone against their will, especially those that are different from them which includes the civil noble constitution. The purpose is to ensure that supernatural beings learn to gain the interest or attention of others without the use of force but with good behaviour. If they repel the interest or attention of others given the hostile nature of the supernatural constitutions, they need to know in order to adjust their behaviour rather than force themselves on others and live in delusion at the risk of self-destruction.

The threat to the implementation of the civilized legal regulation is the supernatural constitution, the weak link to the creation of a properly constituted police service, bribery and corruption; the currency is barbarism, only appeals to the supernatural constitution because of its uncivilized nature. Whether they are supernatural beings that consider themselves family or companions of the civil noble constitutions they pose a serious threat to the security and role of the civil noble constitution as ruler, this is why the law, domestic and international legislations, do not accept any relationships with supernatural beings outside the predetermined guidelines in common law.

The supernatural constitution likes a bit of rough and is willing to compromise the civilized legal regulation to accommodate their natural barbaric urges. These urges are very serious when they go as far as suspending heaven or civilization, advocating a route involving torture, self-harm, the unlawful condemnation of the civil noble constitution to hell.

A bit of compromise here and a bit of compromise there, the essence of policing, the police service, is lost, the safeguard is the standard, the foundation, the essence of policing, the civil noble constitution as a constant reminder.

Compromises in some cases referred to as jokes and games

Regulation

by supernatural beings will create lawlessness, hell on earth, it serves no purpose to deny that the supernatural constitution is hostile. Common law recognizes the seriousness of the harmful effects of the lawless hostile supernatural constitution if unchecked, as a consequence the rights and privileges of the civil noble constitution and the protocols regarding supernatural beings communicating or having contact with the civil noble constitution.

These protocols, rights and privileges of the civil noble constitution are integral components of the civilized legal regulation.

This regulation does not permit unhealthy supernatural manipulations of your health because they want to influence a decision or force you into a meeting etcetera. The supernatural constitution wants to retain an unlawful control of someone's life directly or indirectly by force but the comedy is that they want to make it appear voluntary. Science is used to create a civilization using the civil noble constitution as the standard, used to bridge the gap between the civil and supernatural constitutions without compromising the civil noble constitution. All scientific inventions in order to comply with the rule, the standard, must be safe, must meet the requirements of accessibility, usability and durability using the civil noble constitution as the standard. This eliminates the need for the use of supernatural powers and senses. The civilization must be established for supernatural beings to have met their obligations to the state, this eliminates the need for forced manual labour of supernatural beings without the disruptive use of supernatural powers and senses.

There are a lot of imitations of the civilized legal regulation used by supernatural beings for organized unlawful barbarisms.

It is a serious crime, a crime against humanity, for a supernatural being to pretend to be of a civil noble constitution for the purpose of ruling. Ruling is sacred for peaceful regulatory purposes and is not compatible with the supernatural constitution whether or not the supernatural being is pretending to be of a civil noble constitution.

The supernatural constitution likes a bit of rough, danger, savagery, challenges or obstacles, which are not compatible with real regulation. The supernatural constitution will opt for hostile methods for solutions to problems that in all likelihood they are responsible for, a vicious circle.

The civilized legal regulation, the police service, operates under ideal conditions with very limited applications because the correct identification, interpretation and application of the law serve as a significant deterrent to the commission of a crime.

The civilized legal regulation, the police service, is a sacred scientific method of keeping the peace, the provision of goods and services, the apprehension of the supernatural criminal. It provides an organized way of delivering international peace and security, goods and services.

The objective of the civilized legal regulation, the police service, is to give rest, to create the necessary conditions to

have a relaxed easy stress free life.
The supernatural political lawless regulation supports a supernatural political culture that creates conditions for some people to have an advantage over others. The supernatural political regulation creates words like charity, help or aids, making some people feel important at the expense of others. Death, illnesses, ageing, poverty, supernatural political phenomena integral to a supernatural political culture, a political lawless standard beyond the capabilities of the civil noble constitution, laws, common law, international and domestic legislations expressly forbid the participation of the civil noble constitution in these supernatural political systems or cultures. The sacred determination has been made that given the fact that the civil noble constitution has been sacredly constituted to represent a completely different school of thought or ideology or way of life, any direct or indirect participation of the civil noble constitution in the supernatural political system or culture is by force, the manipulation of supernatural powers and senses by supernatural beings.
All versions of the afterlife, afterlife plans, are not compatible with the civil noble constitution, they are beyond the capabilities of the civil noble constitution, they will unlawfully render the civil noble constitution insane and force an unlawful dependency on the supernatural constitution. They are unlawful under the civilized legal regulation, they are racist.
Uncertainty or confusion or disorientation are supernatural

attacks on the civil noble constitution, to undermine the civilized legal regulation, to make the civil noble constitution dependent on supernatural beings and the supernatural political regulation.

Supernatural beings play games with death, illnesses, ageing evidenced in the supernatural alterations to films and music, with graphic fighting, death scenes and in some African films graphic scenes of the misuse of supernatural powers to make people ill, some supernatural phenomena that have not yet been registered as diseases with names. This accounts for the undermining of law and order, the supernatural political regulation playing games with governance.

Under the supernatural political regulations there are changes to your body, constitution, to align you with whichever supernatural political party is in government, these changes affect you psychologically.

The sacred objective of the civilized legal regulation is to give rest, to have a relaxed attitude to life. Why the rush? In a real civilization, this does not include stopping the creation of a civilization; the creation of a civilization must be done quickly. The civil noble constitution has been sacredly constituted to be allergic to uncivilized living conditions, to be impatient for the creation of a real civilization. Uncivilized living conditions are torturous for the civil noble constitution. Something very funny, dumb criminal syndrome, supernatural beings of African and Asian origins in the West believe that they have the licence to subject the civil noble constitution of African origin to supernatural racist attacks, the civilized legal regulation does not notice skin colour, regulates supernatural behaviour, prevents any type of racist supernatural attack on the civil noble constitution regardless of the skin colour of the supernatural being.

In the star trek drama series and films by Gene Roddenberry, fiction, the character Data does not get the punchline of a joke because of the way he is constituted, he is an android; it makes no sense to have an unprofessional attitude with the character Data as a consequence. Supernatural beings are always attracted to the unique nature of the civil noble constitution when I am accessing public services and try to be unprofessional, their barbaric way of socializing which always ends badly because they do not get it, it is because of the civil noble constitution that professionalism is the law, they, supernatural beings are too uncivilized for any other type of interaction with the civil noble constitution. The civilized legal regulation does not permit unlawful contact or interaction with the civil noble constitution, does not allow the civil noble constitution to suffer in silence from the barbaric attempts at jokes and games by supernatural beings. The difference between the fictional character Data and the civil noble constitution is that the pointless attempts are at the expense of the physical and mental wellbeing of the civil noble constitution.

An important component of the civilized legal regulation is the official distinction of the civil noble constitution as a law lord, a common law requirement, a requirement in the bible; this ensures that the identity of the civil noble constitution is

Regulation

not political but legal, not dependent on the goodwill of supernatural beings.

Under the civilized legal regulation the civil noble constitution is the standard for regulatory purposes, beings whose mental capacities are below or above this regulatory standard are mentally retarded and in need of the guidance of the law.

The current use of information is racist, only supernatural beings are aware of important information, for example, the universe and the existence of other civilizations. There is a difference between withholding information to protect the civil noble constitution from supernatural phenomena and lying. The civilized legal regulation requires information about important issues to be shared fairly, in a civilized way. The civil noble constitution has the highest security clearance for regulatory purposes.

The nature of the supernatural constitution is as such that it has the inability to distinguish between a hostile condition or situation and a non-hostile condition or situation, some mistake this for strength, but it is a breach of security, a weak link; the civilized legal regulation, the police service, must ensure that the supernatural constitution because of the way it is constituted does not put off for tomorrow what should be done today, in order not to put lives in danger.

The supernatural political regulations are based on a false reality, they allow supernatural beings to bug the vulnerable with dust, cobwebs, cracks etcetera that are linked to the natural with no scientific connection to the natural, they are supernatural phenomena attempts by supernatural beings to create their idea of reality, reality that must have problems to be considered normal. The civilized legal regulation forbids the unlawful misuse of supernatural powers and senses to bug the vulnerable in the guise of help, natural phenomena etcetera; as a consequence the vulnerable nature of the civil noble constitution regulates living conditions and activities of supernatural beings. The civil vulnerable nature of the noble lord regulates the activities of supernatural beings reinforced by the sacred determination that the civil noble lord must be distinguished officially as ruler, law lord.

The civilized legal regulation ensures that for regulatory purposes the supernatural powers and senses of supernatural beings are recreated scientifically and used scientifically, scientific methods, to compensate for the differences between the civil and supernatural constitutions. What can be done supernaturally should also be done scientifically; examples are the replication and regeneration technologies in the star trek science fiction drama series and movies by Gene Roddenberry. Regeneration and replication were mentioned in the bible but they should be done legally scientifically and not supernaturally. Necessity is the mother of invention. This need to compensate for the differences between the civil and supernatural constitutions scientifically with scientific inventions creates a civilization. A civilization or state is an extension of the civil noble constitution. Unfortunately science is being used unlawfully to cause harm rather than to support life, which started with the tree that produced the forbidden fruit in the Garden of Eden. Things manufactured or produced like food, cars, planes, energies for heating and light, gas and electricity, are hazardous or dangerous. They reflect the dangerous nature of the supernatural constitution.

The references to the civil noble constitution as a being born of God as a distinction between the civil and supernatural constitutions, identify the civil noble constitution as ruler, naturally righteous, the investigations of crimes against the civil noble constitution are not based on fiction or a false reality or role plays but are based on the truth, the source or causes of crime.

The propagandists will interpret the civilized legal regulation, an advanced monarchy, a dictatorship; the interpretation of the civilized legal regulation as a dictatorship, oppressive, is misleading because of the purpose of the civilized legal regulation, the recipient and the dictator. The recipients of the regulations are supernatural beings and the dictator or instructor is the civil noble constitution, about what constitutes civilized behaviour.

If every supernatural being offended or attacked by another supernatural being wants to react or retaliate it could be very disruptive in a society, the bible instructs that vengeance is the Lord's, this means that it must be a coordinated or organized effort to apprehend and punish offenders through the police service.

The police service is the modern or an advanced type of monarchy; it is the civilized legal regulation that prevents

Regulation

supernatural beings from forcing themselves on the vulnerable under the guises of angels and demons against their will by exploiting the problems they unlawfully created in the lives of the vulnerable. The civilized legal regulation prevents supernatural beings from exploiting the vulnerable, using the vulnerable as projects to create activities for themselves, by ensuring that there are constant problems in the lives of the vulnerable even when these problems are preventable.

Regulation

3. The state

Regulation

The state is the extension of the civil noble constitution; the civilization is used to cater to the needs of the civil noble constitution through science, technological advancements. The use of the civil noble constitution as the standard, the use of science to redress the imbalance in the differences between the civil and supernatural constitutions creates a civilization, the state.

This is like terraforming, the creation of a civilization to make a planet able to sustained human life through science. It is astonishing that the planet earth is not currently able to sustain human life because of the wickedness of the supernatural constitution.

The effectiveness of a state is its ability to regulate the activities of supernatural beings. The current crisis in the world regarding the god complex of the supernatural constitution, the impossibility of catering to the need of the supernatural constitution to play god, all supernatural beings believing that they are above the law, resulting in hell on earth.

All activities that undermine the effectiveness of the state, like religion, that advocates the supremacy of the supernatural constitution blatantly compromises the principle of the state, establish lawlessness.

The understanding of the meaning of the law or standard or rule given the differences between the civil and supernatural constitutions will make a mockery of the activities of supernatural beings that have undermined the sacredness of governance.

The underdeveloped state of science and technology in the world is as a consequence of the hostile nature of the supernatural constitution, a conspiracy to undermine the effectiveness of the state; it maintains the prostitution culture in place at present. In some cases that the current stage of science and technology offers assistance, for example healthcare (exercise and fitness), medication, and security etcetera are sabotaged by supernatural beings to create dependency and worship.

Science and technology offer life and independence which the supernatural constitution deliberately compromises or undermines choosing to take the place of science and technology, to have a more direct involvement or contact, which is not compatible with the hostile nature of the supernatural constitution. The supernatural constitution is volatile, when things go wrong, as they inevitably will, the victim, the civil noble constitution, is blamed, stranded and enslaved. This creates emotional entanglements which put the health and life of the civil noble constitution in danger from the misuse of supernatural powers and senses; they try to do the forbidden, to draw the civil noble constitution into their world of barbarism intentionally and unintentionally as a consequence of supernatural perceptions of the supernatural constitution.

The scientific method or formula for supernatural beings to contact or communicate with the civil noble constitution are underestimated by supernatural beings, the sacred protocols, the rights and privileges of the civil noble constitution create the state. These sacred protocols for contact or communication with the civil noble constitution, the rights and privileges of the civil noble constitution regulate the actions of supernatural beings as a consequence protect the civil noble constitution from the uncivilized nature of the supernatural constitution.

The references made to supernatural beings in the bible were in the forms of God, angels, demons and the devil; they had separate existence from the civil noble constitution referred to as man. The instructions to supernatural beings referred to as angels were to improve the living conditions of the civil noble constitution. What does this mean? Was it to make man worship them? Does this mean direct or indirect torture? Was it to make man subservient to them? Was it to introduce diseases, poverty, death, ageing into the life of man? What is the time limit of the intervention? These instructions or Christian teachings were always going to be vulnerable to barbarism, misapplication, misinterpretation. They were always going to be vulnerable to the misinterpretation of unrestricted access to or interference with the civil noble constitution. Do you terraform the individual or the land?

Supernatural beings have gone round in circles, explored every option but the right one, the complete submission to the law, the civil noble constitution, man. What do you want? The simple coronation of man as the standard.

This simple direction has been misapplied, used unlawfully to subject man to attempts at ritual humiliation, used to establish conflicting ideologies or warfare with man caught in the middle, used unlawfully for barbaric activities that cater to the hostile nature of the supernatural constitution at the expense of law and order. All these problems are as a consequence of the supernatural constitution's refusal to accept its hostile nature, living in denial at the expense of law and order.

The state provides everything its inhabitants need, food, water, services, shelter (housing), security (the police service), transportation etcetera. All natural resources belong to the state or are part of the state.

Science and technology and the law give life to supernatural beings, they help supernatural beings exercise self-control, help to eliminate godlike or god complex traits, encourage individualism.

The law, science and technology ennoble supernatural beings and create a real civilized society.

It is funny that supernatural beings associate being godlike in the proper legal sense with the show of supernatural powers and senses, supernaturalism, on the contrary, to be godlike legally is to be law abiding, civilized .

Processes or procedures or protocols, scientific methods that provide security from supernatural powers and senses are being used abusively by saboteurs in political supernatural role plays. The purpose is to discredit law and order or scientific methods in favour of lawless oppressive supernatural methods. The supernatural phenomena diseases or illnesses have been used politically to favour supernatural lawless methods; processes or procedures, scientific methods that are only used for good purposes are being used or applied to the supernatural phenomena diseases or illnesses giving lifespan to these supernatural phenomena as duration or process to undermine the concept of law and order and the scientific method.

In the United Kingdom, common law, tradition has tried to accommodate the needs of the supernatural and civil constitutions, the working class and the nobility, a compromise; unfortunately this has proven unsuccessful because of the unreasonableness of the supernatural political working class. The constant misuse of supernatural powers and senses by supernatural beings to encroach on the freedoms of the nobility.

The state cannot make compromises, the supernatural constitution is volatile susceptible to uncivilized behaviour, so if allowed to engage in uncivilized behaviour, for example, eating meat, to be carnivorous, it will get out of control and threaten the king's peace in a civilized society.

The sadistic nature of the supernatural constitution is evidenced with these examples of supernatural attacks on the civil noble constitution; some cultures have been smoking something similar to cigarettes before it became commercialized. Given the nature of the supernatural constitution and the nature of the civil noble constitution, selling cigarettes which have always been regulated by governments, the supernatural constitution would have been aware if they were suitable for human consumption, that they were or are extremely addictive, that they were and are poisonous. So the determination will be made that supernatural beings deliberately conspired to get the nobles to smoke cigarettes, by castings spells on real nobles, with the intention of revealing that they are poisonous on cigarette packets, knowing that the nobles are under spells of addiction to cigarettes, a torturous effect for real nobles. Sexual intercourse is natural, a civil right for real nobles, a natural healthy addiction like food, which has been supernaturally compromised and made a poisonous experience for real nobles only, given the differences between the civil and supernatural constitutions.

This is a deliberate compromise of the purpose and function of the state. The state is sacred and cannot be party to the mental and physical harm of its law abiding citizens directly or indirectly.

It is important to note that diseases or illnesses are not natural but supernatural phenomena associated with the deliberate misuse of supernatural powers and senses. It is the same thing as being told that if you have a companion or touch a product or something that you will be killed or murdered. There is a legitimate reason why all laws bar supernatural beings from any type of association with the civil noble constitution. In limited circumstances that contact is allowed there are strict sacred protocols in order to protect the civil noble constitution, reinforced by the sacred rights and privileges of the civil noble constitution. This is similar to an abusive parent of a child being permitted to visit that child

under strict supervision.
There has to be a fair distribution of the state's resource for regulatory purposes, the legislations do not recognize the supernatural constitution's right to own property or to have access to state services for regulatory purposes. They can only have what a properly constituted state allows them to have for regulatory purposes.
The value, preservation and support of life are the essential components of the purpose and function of the state. The state is undermined when any of these components is compromised.
Supernatural methods undermine the value for life given the oppressive or domineering nature of the supernatural constitution. The sacred determination has been made about supernaturalism when Lady Eve was created for Lord Adam when he was shielded from it. The show of power, supernatural powers and senses, has a bullying intimidating effect on those that are different from supernatural beings like the civil noble constitution. Scientific methods through science and technology can adequately replace the need for the use of supernatural powers and senses.
Given the sacred determination made about the civil noble constitution and what the civil noble constitution represents it is strange when supernatural beings want to regulate the actions of the civil noble constitution supernaturally. Why? The civil noble constitution is righteous, for supernatural beings to claim moral superiority over the righteous they need to regulate the righteous even when there is nothing to

regulate. This will require the manipulation of supernatural powers and senses to create situations to justify intervening supernaturally, to prove the superiority of supernatural methods or interventions. The purpose of the law, the civil noble constitution, will suggest, cutting off your nose to spite your face mentality.

The former Soviet Union proved the possibility of the creation of a real civilization, the state, a fair system of equality, with some adjustments to create the perfect civilization. The missing essential component was the truth, the truth about the supernatural constitution, the regulation of the supernatural constitution, lifespan, the state being an extension of the civil noble constitution as ruler, the standard.

Supernatural methods, plans and solutions are traumatic, aggressive, and unnecessarily dramatic, a reflection of the hostile aggressive nature of the supernatural constitution, this is why they are not allowed to contact, communicate or associate with the civil noble constitution. The laws, common law, international and domestic legislations have made provisions already for the civil noble constitution, which eliminates the need for supernatural methods, plans or solutions in the life of the civil noble constitution. Although supernatural beings have tried unsuccessfully to compromise or undermine the provisions already made for the civil noble constitution by law, the simplistic option, in favour of the supernatural dramatic aggressive or hostile methods, plans or solutions.

Regulation

An example of a state economy was the economy developed by the former Soviet Union, if applied properly truthfully eradicates inequality, poverty, lawlessness etcetera. This type of economy makes regulation possible and effective. For regulatory purposes this economy is supported by the single currency concept not just in Europe but the rest of the world. The former Soviet Union's type of state economy gets better with technological advancements.

The market economy which has overtaken or replaced the state economy in the world is a reflection of an insane wicked world. The market economy encourages discrimination, inequality and the undermining of the state. The market economy is a threat to state security. The stock market which is part of the market economy like gambling gives an unfair advantage to the supernatural constitution.

It is interesting that the former Soviet Union banned political and religious activities, there were media restrictions; they were considered threats to national security.

The scientific methods of passing on information to meet the needs of the civil noble constitution serve regulatory purposes, provide security, and help with the creation of a real civilization.

It is not possible to breach the peace of supernatural beings if they do not feel threatened by most of the actions of their peers. For the purposes of national security, the standard for regulation is the civil noble constitution who will feel threatened by all antisocial supernatural activities.

The nature of the supernatural constitution makes it possible to know what goes on in the privacy of a home like sexual intercourse, they, supernatural beings, then believe that they can recreate sexual intercourse in films as if the supernatural constitution is the standard, they see it supernaturally so it makes no difference to recreate it in films. The unlawfully altered state of films means you are subjected to live sex shows at the expense of a good story. The standard is the civil noble constitution who cannot see what goes on in the privacy of a home.

When someone says that their profession requires them to have sexual intercourse with different people, as is the case in films, it sounds a bit like prostitution. This is an example of the loss of inhibitions being applied negatively self-destructively. About a century ago when the concept of a film or movie was at its infancy or development gruesome violence and sex scenes were not necessary to tell a story.

It is impossible to tell the truth amidst this level of lawlessness without it appearing confrontational, it is not the intention, it is a contribution to help establish a proper civilization.

Unfortunately I am being attacked supernaturally, a type of supernatural regulation, for telling the truth, I am being made to feel ill.

Tradition, common law, has made the determination that political cultures and systems only apply to the political constitution because of its limitations and not the legal constitution. The supernatural constitution is a political constitution because of its limitations; it is uncivilized because of its supernatural powers and senses. The civil noble constitution is a legal constitution with no limitations because of the lack of supernatural powers and senses.

The state through the civil noble constitution as ruler, the standard, provides the necessary conditions to free the supernatural constitution from supernatural political lawless systems and cultures.

Supernatural beings are not constituted to be rulers; they were and are puppets for supernatural beings to maintain the status quo of lawlessness. A real ruler has to have been sacredly constituted to be of a civil noble constitution from birth, whose sacred self-interest is to establish and maintain real law and order, a real civilization, a state.

The political supernatural blue capitalist ideology is a fraudulent use of the standard derived from the administrative nature of the civil noble constitution, its correct use is the enforcement of the prime directive to protect the legal status of the civil noble constitution, the civil noble constitution should not be compromised or altered in order to maintain the sacred standard of law and order through the civil noble constitution. It is being used by supernatural beings to undermine the state by the privatization of limited natural resources; keeping public wealth or resources in the hands of a few while the majority languish in poverty or struggle to make ends meet. They used it to create inhumane conditions requiring a lot of people to compete for limited resources. Creating a culture of hate and envy, the competitive culture, survival of the fittest, the strong oppressing the weak, the misuse of supernatural powers and senses by supernatural beings to maintain superiority over the civil noble constitution.

The companions of the civil noble constitution are ladies; the sacred requirement of the companions of the civil noble lord to be virgins amongst supernatural females is as a consequence of the delicate nature of the civil noble constitution and the corruptibility of the supernatural constitution or susceptibility of the supernatural constitution to barbarism. It is easier and sustainable to make a virgin a lady, a suitable companion for the civil noble lord. This sacred requirement helps to ensure the security of the state. Although, it is important to note, it is unlawful for any supernatural female to refuse the sexual advances of the civil noble constitution.

The education and training of the civil noble constitution as outlined by common law, United Kingdom tradition and traditions of other countries, are based on the reality of the differences between the civil and supernatural constitutions, the truth, done with care and respect for the dignity of person regulating the uncivilized nature of the supernatural constitution. This process builds the confidence of the ruler and state or national security.

Politics or democracy, religions advocate the supremacy of the supernatural constitution over the state, the civil noble constitution, creating anarchy, lawlessness. They advocate challenging the prime directive, the supremacy of the state, the civil noble constitution, and establishing disorder in the guise of democracy, supernatural political systems of government.

The objective of these supernatural political lawless systems is to replace one type of anxiety with another; the comedy is that the constitution that is most susceptible to the anxiety effect, the civil noble constitution, is the constitution sacredly exempt from the supernatural political systems and their effects. The sacred determination made is that the destabilizing effects of these political systems should be on supernatural beings and not civil beings. To undermine this sacred determination will attract serious consequences or punishments for the offenders.

It does not suit the supernatural constitution for living conditions to be perfect, civilized. This is evidenced by the wrong interpretation of the Christian teachings to create hell on earth, the supernatural political systems of government as solutions to problems they have created, poverty, death, illnesses ageing etcetera. Supernatural methods or interventions are misleading, they thrive on indefinite crisis. The state requires distinction or identification of its rulers, the process of identification or distinction must be done in a proper way that reflects that the standard is the civil noble constitution. The official residence of rulers or ministers are refurbished or maintained regularly by a state department because it is expected that the employees of the state department have gone through the necessary training and security checks to have access to the civil noble constitution or the property or properties of the civil noble constitution.

This sacred requirement is as a consequence of the hostile nature of the supernatural constitution and the delicate civil nature of the civil noble constitution. The distinction or identification of the civil noble constitution as a law lord is a sacred requirement because whether supernatural beings pretend to be of civil noble constitutions or not they are not of civil noble constitutions, to treat both constitutions as if they are the same puts the health and life of the civil noble constitution in serious danger because of the delicate nature of the civil noble constitution.

The bible made the sacred determination that the recovery from supernatural attacks, illnesses or diseases, must be instantaneous for the civil noble constitution and provisions must be in place to comply with this sacred determination. This sacred determination prevents the unlawful torture of the civil noble constitution with illnesses or diseases; the determination was made with the sacred understanding that it is possible to treat any type of supernatural attack. The sacred determination was applied to the civil noble constitution unconditionally; this is the case because the civil noble constitution is righteous naturally regardless of the manipulations or misuse of supernatural powers and senses by supernatural beings to compromise the righteousness of the civil noble constitution.

The institution of the state with the correct identification, interpretation and application of the law is to enforce the sacred determination that prevention is better than cure.

Regulation

Regulation

4. Author's notes

Regulation

The supernatural regulation has always been about interfering with a being supernaturally with or without their consent to fit into the plans of the supernatural being or beings. These plans always involve the compromise of life or health, the dramatic effect, consistent with the hostile nature of the supernatural constitution.

I am of a civil noble constitution; the righteousness of the civil noble constitution was news to me after years of deceit, the realization that those around me were different from me with supernatural powers and senses, concealing the truth while advocating the worship of the supernatural constitution. This means that my development started when I became aware of the differences by my efforts, meaning that I am decades behind my supernatural age-mates.

This suggests a culture of direct and indirect hostility toward the civil noble constitution by supernatural beings regardless of their age or gender or skin colour.

These abuses take the forms of jokes, games and relationships.

This book examines whether it is the supernatural uncivilized constitution or the civil noble constitution that regulates human behaviour. It is important that the method for the apprehension or arrest of the supernatural criminal is not confused with the appropriate method of regulation.

The clarity of information and purpose, the effective provision of services using the civil noble constitution as the standard as a method of regulation is examined in this book. The consent of the sacred regulator, the law lord, the

Regulation

standard, the civil noble constitution, cannot be obtained by direct or indirect force to establish a police service. The creation of a properly constituted police service must be in the best interest of the law lord, the sacred regulator, the standard, the civil noble constitution. It is a sacred decision by the sacred regulator if repelled or repulsed by the actions of supernatural beings, a failure by supernatural beings to behave appropriately, to behave in a civilized manner. Regulation requires that the protocols, rights and privileges are instituted or correct from the start, relationships or associations that were conceived from an abusive or unlawful foundation will remain the same way for the duration of the relationship or association. In cases that the relationship or association involves the civil noble constitution, the unlawful or abusive foundation will be at the expense of the mental and physical wellbeing of the civil noble constitution with severe consequences for the offenders, supernatural beings.

This book confirms that all supernatural political regulations are used to undermine or compromise the state, the civil noble constitution, as if competing for moral superiority over the civil noble constitution. The prosperity of supernatural beings is obtained at the expense of the security of the state, law and order, and at the expense of the wellbeing of the vulnerable.

Unfortunately supernatural rulers are political, puppets, in this lawless culture, so consciously or subconsciously, directly or indirectly, supernatural beings treat the sacred legal ruler, the civil noble constitution, as a puppet. The civil noble lord has been sacredly constituted to be different from supernatural beings, to make being a puppet impossible.

In this lawless system, supernatural political regulations, all services, shops, supermarkets, films, music, taxis etcetera are tainted with lawlessness, but the civil noble constitution is the only constitution that retains the legal right to use these services or products. Why? The civil noble constitution is a sacred regulator, these services or products are to be corrected to suit the sacred nature of the civil noble constitution, the sacred regulator, like an undercover police officer. The law does not permit refusing the civil noble constitution access to or the use of any service.

Supernatural beings cannot have direct or indirect political relationships with the civil noble constitution, law lord, the relationships or associations must be legal.

Supernatural beings cannot obtain directly or indirectly by force or deception the services of the law.

Science is an extension of the civil noble constitution, as a consequence can only be used for good beneficial purposes; it should not be hazardous to the civil noble constitution like the apple tree in the Garden of Eden.

In my books including this book are deductions or conclusions any reasonable person would make given the differences between the civil and supernatural constitutions, although these conclusions or deductions are confirmed in the bible, common law, international and domestic legislations, for a real lawyer to work out.

Regulation

Unfortunately supernatural beings are in the habit of compromising a regulator or regulation because they are too barbaric or uncivilized to be law abiding, they are a serious constant threat to the security of the civil noble lord.
All supernatural rulers are puppets, whether they are referred to as monarchs, military rulers, politicians. Supernatural rulers are puppets, because of how they are constituted maintain organized barbarisms or lawlessness; they maintain the status quo regardless of appearances. They are supernatural manipulations to undermine real law and order. Unfortunately, as a consequence they do not know how to deal with the reality of a real sacred or anointed ruler, the civil noble constitution. It appears that the vulnerabilities of the civil noble constitution make the civil lord susceptible to supernatural manipulations, a better puppet; on the contrary, the vulnerabilities make the civil noble constitution immune to being a puppet or supernatural political manipulations.
The incentive for good scientific inventions should not be financial rewards to have a better life than somebody else but to have a better life through the state, by improving the state. John F Kennedy, a former president of the United States of America said to ask not what your country can do for you but to ask for what you can do for your country.
It is natural to be self-centred, self-preservation even at the expense of the wellbeing of others, this is why the state eliminates dependency, the state represents independence, individual rights and personal freedoms.

Science, the garden of Eden, a tree is created or planted, lives or stands forever, this is the natural lifespan of the tree unless obstructed unnaturally.

The bible or Christian teachings instruct that forever or immortality as the lifespan using the civil noble constitution as the standard to create paradise as the sacred living condition, the teachings further instruct that alterations to the living condition constitute hell or punishment.

All civilizations in Europe, Japan and China, the United States of America achieved their level of civilization through the unity of the monarchy type government, the state government principle before the introduction of the divisive concept of politics or democracy. Although the civilizations are not of the required standard, they demonstrate the possibilities of a real state government with the civil noble constitution. It also demonstrates the problems the countries referred to as third world countries are experiencing trying to establish civilizations through politics rather than the state. Unity or collectivism for political supernatural lawless purposes is wrong but unity or collectivism for legal purposes creates individualism, individual rights and personal freedoms and the state.

When you have supernatural beings claiming moral superiority over each other, different political lawless affiliations, claiming unlawfully the right to determine the affairs of the civil noble constitution, when all supernatural political affiliations constitute breaches of the security of the civil noble constitution, undermine the creation of a real civilization, the state.

The holier than thou attitudes of supernatural beings toward the civil noble constitution reinforced by references to the uncivilized components of their supernatural constitutions as righteous are to undermine any attempt to regulate them. Attempts to regulate supernatural beings are referred to as demonic; the civil noble constitution as a consequence is referred to as demonic and not righteous. This is similar to a virus or toxin referring to attempts to destroy or control them as demonic and doctors as devils.

Regulation is meeting the needs of the civil noble constitution which includes bringing supernatural beings under control through the establishment of the state, a bit like sectioning supernatural beings under the mental health Act to prevent supernatural beings from being dangerous to themselves and dangerous to others.

Supernatural beings are barred by law from direct or indirect communication or contact with the civil noble lord, international and domestic legislations do not recognize the supernatural constitution for any type of legal interaction with the civil noble lord. Common law identifies the reason as barbarism, the supernatural constitution is barbaric, uncivilized and a danger to the civil noble lord if unregulated. As a consequence common law has provided strict guidelines in the event of any contact or communication with the civil noble lord for the protection of the civil noble lord which serve regulatory purposes. The civil noble constitution has been constituted deliberately to be delicate and allergic to barbarism. So when supernatural beings undermine or ignore the sacred strict guidelines for contact or communication with the civil noble lord the effect given the differences between the civil and supernatural constitutions is to make the life of the civil noble lord hell unlawfully triggering the sacred legal right of vengeance of the civil noble lord, the condemnation to hell of the wicked. Ignoring these guidelines regarding contact or communication is similar to somebody who has a deadly infection to knowingly infect others with the disease when it can be avoided.

Under the lawless supernatural regulations, plans, methods, the route to heaven under their interpretation of the Christian teachings, all their endgames avoid addressing the real issue, the real issue or crisis is the immediate effective regulation of the supernatural constitution. Avoidance of the real issue or crisis ensures that lawlessness the problem remains constant, maintaining the status quo, the supremacy of the supernatural constitution at the expense of law and order. Power tripping, cutting off their noses to spite their faces. These are reflections of the barbaric nature of the supernatural constitution.

Unity under the state principle unlike the political principle, does not mean the loss of privacy, an open unregulated relationship with those around you, on the contrary, it provides privacy, individual rights, regulated relationships with those around you. For the state principle to work the supernatural constitution must be identified and regulated, requiring that a distinction between the civil and

Regulation

supernatural constitutions be made officially for regulatory purposes.

Bridging the gap between the civil and supernatural constitutions through science and technology, technological advancements, establishes the state or civilization and regulates the supernatural constitution. This sacred determination confirms the civil noble constitution as a sacred regulator, direct and indirect, that the civil noble lord is a commissioner of police, a law lord.

The nature of the supernatural constitution confirms acquiescence with the lawless political system or systems of government in the world, the political lawless regulation is based on a lie, whether or not the supernatural being is directly involved they protect the lie by not telling the truth in a proper civilized manner. The civil noble constitution however cannot acquiesce with a political system that is based on lie, a lie that operates under supernatural political role plays beyond the capabilities of the civil noble lord.

Under the civilized legal regulation, the truth eliminates the need for the use of violence or force in most part, two or more liars cannot claim moral superiority over the other, the lack of moral justification, lies, creates the breeding ground for violence when a group of liars claim moral superiority over another group of liars, terraforming the planet to suit the barbaric nature of the supernatural constitution at the expense of peace and security.

You need to be of a civil noble constitution to know that the barring of supernatural beings from contact or communication with the civil noble constitution is very serious, strict. The references to this in the bible were made in the form of angels and demons, supernatural beings, having a separate existence from man, common law also made references to this in the form of the working class and the nobility not socializing, separate existence. The nobility representing the civil noble constitution and the working class representing supernatural beings, the bible reinforcing this sacred determination by insisting that only law abiding supernatural beings, referred to as angels, can have contact or communicate with the civil noble constitution. The bible provided the guidelines; it is for supernatural beings to work out what it means to be law abiding supernatural beings, referred to as angels.

Supernatural beings create hostile living conditions to suit their barbaric wicked constitutions at the expense of law and order, peace and security. This is further emphasized in the bible with the reference to the counsel of the wicked, the ungodly, this includes the wicked interpretation and application of the Christian teachings, the wicked interpretation and application of policing, the wicked interpretation and application of companionship, the wicked interpretation and application of heaven etcetera. This is similar but worse than the Klingons a fictional alien species in the star trek drama series and films by Gene Roddenberry, a species that consider total anarchy as an honourable way of living.

As a consequence of being unregulated supernatural beings

Regulation

subject me to constant psychological attacks, racist attacks, your concerns about something, like a phobia, are being always used as weapons to attack you deliberately while making it appear to be coincidental while pretending to be of civil constitutions, even though they are not of civil constitutions. It is even more sadistic when it is obvious that the phobia or concern is as a consequence of the misuse of supernatural powers and senses by supernatural beings. You can never know peace when supernatural beings develop this type of retarded barbaric interest in you; this type of racist attack is more pronounced with white supernatural beings. Does this make white supernatural beings demons? The viciousness of their attacks on the vulnerable, the civil noble constitution, will suggest that they are genetically demonic. The use of religion, governance to proclaim themselves superior to other races, taking responsibility for the complete lawlessness in the world, the divisive nature of democracy, will suggest that they are demons.

This apparent genetic defect can be reversed through regulation, strict adherence to medication, the correct identification, interpretation and application of the law. The elimination of anti-regulatory practices, barbarisms, like homosexuality, carnivorous practices, the persecution of the law lord, politics or democracy etcetera, will help to reverse or get under control the genetic defect.

When supernatural beings while pretending to be of civil constitutions, legal persons, make determinations about what constitutes an attack on the legal person, are breaches of the security of the civil noble constitution and violations of the rights of the legal person under article 3 of the universal declaration of human rights and article 6 of the international convention on civil and political rights. The nature of the supernatural constitution will make supernatural beings downplay what will normally constitute serious attacks on the legal person undermining the security of the legal person. Under supernatural political regulations, the civil noble constitution has to be compromised, discredited, for supernatural beings to have unrestricted access to the civil noble constitution; the civil noble constitution has to be condemned to hell unlawfully to fit into supernatural political role plays. The false realities, supernatural political role plays indirectly condemn the civil noble constitution to hell unlawfully ending in the direct unlawful condemnation to hell of the civil noble constitution. The civil noble constitution under these supernatural regulations will always fall short of the standard set by supernatural beings inviting regular supernatural attacks. These supernatural attacks constitute what is considered by supernatural beings to be jokes, games, relationships, companionships or socializing, sexual intercourse or love making etcetera.

For this sacred concept regulation, policing, to operate properly or correctly, the sacred concept of the separation of powers must be strictly adhered to for the creation and maintenance of regulation or policing, the administration of justice. The sacred concept of the separation of powers identifies the civil noble lord as law lord, commissioner of

police and supernatural beings that have attained the necessary sacred qualification to assist the civil noble lord as law enforcement officers. There are sacred tests and sacred security measures to ensure that supernatural beings do not encroach on the sacred authority of the civil noble lord.
The reason why the state, the civilized legal regulation, and not the uncivilized supernatural regulation, investigates, apprehends or detains criminals is that there must be a recorded legal reason, this is why science and technology are the legal options and not supernaturalism. This is based on the verification of criminal responsibility, which is not susceptible to witch hunts, the demonic bugging effect.
The common law rights and privileges of the civil noble lord, the common law protocols regarding contact or communication with the civil noble lord are all laws that regulate supernatural beings, the sacred confirmation of the civil noble lord as law lord, sacred regulator.
Civil rights or the king's rights are like disability rights that exempt the civil noble lord from supernatural political role plays that incorporate death, diseases or illnesses, old age or ageing, hard to get rituals preceding sexual intercourse, poverty, etcetera. This sacred exemption of the civil noble lord is as a consequence of the delicate nature of the civil constitution that serves regulatory purposes.
The expression to clip your wings, confidence because of the nature of the supernatural constitution will lead to power tripping the misuse of supernatural powers and senses; this is also the problem with anger and the supernatural

constitution which will lead to the misuse of supernatural powers and senses. This is not the case with the civil noble constitution; it is a sacred requirement that the civil noble lord be extremely confident, it is essential to regulation given the massive differences between the civil and supernatural constitutions. It is also a sacred requirement for regulatory purposes for the civil noble lord to be angry when provoked or attacked and to have the offenders punished.

Under the wrong interpretation of the Christian teachings, the current practice, supernatural lawless occurrence is considered holy, a godly intervention, under the correct interpretation of the Christian teachings this practice or method is considered unlawful, disruptive in a civilized society. The purpose of regulation is to stop the use of the unholy, ungodly, supernatural method.

Regulation

5. Author's biography

Regulation

My name is Lord Loveday Ememe. I was born in the United Kingdom. I am a graduate of an Anglican seminary school. I graduated from the University of East London with an honours degree in law. I am of a civil noble constitution.

6. Bibliography

Regulation

The Bible

Star trek drama series and films by Gene Roddenberry

www.ingramcontent.com/pod-product-compliance
Lightning Source LLC
Chambersburg PA
CBHW070428180526
45158CB00017B/929